Nature Numbers

CAN YOU SEE A CIRCLE?

Explore Shapes

Ruth A. Musgrave

Children's Press®
An imprint of Scholastic Inc.

Library of Congress Cataloging-in-Publication Data
Names: Musgrave, Ruth A., 1960- author.
Title: Can you see a circle? : explore shapes / Ruth A. Musgrave.
Description: New York : Children's Press, an imprint of Scholastic
  Inc., [2022]. | Series: Nature numbers | Includes index. | Audience:
  Ages 5-7. | Audience: Grades K-1. | Summary: "Nonfiction,
  full-color photos of animals and nature introduce basic math
  concepts and encourage kids to see a world of numbers all
  around them"– Provided by publisher.
Identifiers: LCCN 2021031814 (print) | LCCN 2021031815 (ebook)
  | ISBN 9781338765151 (library binding) | ISBN 9781338765168
  (paperback) | ISBN 9781338765175 (ebk)
Subjects: LCSH: Shapes–Juvenile literature. | Geometry–Juvenile
  literature. | Animals–Miscellanea–Juvenile literature. | BISAC:
  JUVENILE NONFICTION / General | JUVENILE
  NONFICTION / Mathematics / Geometry
Classification: LCC QA445.5 .M88 2022 (print) | LCC QA445.5
  (ebook) | DDC 516/.154–dc23
LC record available at https://lccn.loc.gov/2021031814
LC ebook record available at https://lccn.loc.gov/2021031815

10 9 8 7 6 5 4 3 2 1   22 23 24 25 26

Printed in the U.S.A.   113
First edition, 2022

Series produced by WonderLab Group, LLC
Book design by Moduza Design
Photo editing by Annette Kiesow
Educational consulting by Leigh Hamilton
Copyediting by Jane Sunderland
Proofreading by Molly Reid
Indexing by Connie Binder

Photos ©: cover: Meryll/Dreamstime; 4-5: Lavoview/Dreamstime;
12-13: Anan Butsrimuang/Dreamstime; 14-15: Brian Kushner/
Dreamstime; 18-19: Elina Leonova/Dreamstime; 20-21: Idenviktor/
Dreamstime; 26-27: Brent Coulter/Dreamstime; 28 top right:
Nadya So/Dreamstime; 28 center left: John Hyde/Getty Images;
28 bottom left: Marie-claire Lander/Dreamstime.

All other photos © Shutterstock.

For my best friend, Ampy
—RM

circle

4

Sunflowers <u>sway</u> in a field, yellow and bright.

It's a great day to <u>explore</u> shapes in nature.

Can you see a circle?

sphere

It's a water party!

Drops of <u>dew</u> gather on the leaves. They shimmer in the light. Dew is made of water. Dewdrops are shaped like <u>spheres</u>.

Try It!

A circle is a flat shape.

A sphere is solid like a ball. Look at the dewdrops. Find all the spheres on the leaves.

triangle

Listen!

The sound of chattering birds fills the air. A <u>cardinal</u>'s wing is shaped like a triangle. So is its pointy beak. The cardinal flips leaves and digs in the grass. The search is on for seeds, berries, and wiggly bugs.

Yum!

Try It!

A triangle has three sides and three corners. How many triangle shapes do you see on the bird?

corner

side

Flowers bring the hum of bees.

Bees build row after row of **hexagon** shapes called **honeycombs**. Then they fill each one with tasty honey to eat.

Try It!

One shape can make other shapes. Six triangles can make a hexagon. Count all six sides of the hexagon. Count the triangles.

hexagon

Look!

<u>Boulders</u> form in shapes of all kinds. Wind and weather change them. Do you see a square? So many rocks. So many shapes to find.

Try It!

A square is flat. It has four sides that are the same length. Every square has four corners, too. Point to the sides. Point to the corners.

corner

side

A cube is a solid shape made of six squares. Can you find three things at home that are cubes?

square

Dragonflies spend the day racing through the air. They twist and turn. They fly up and down.

How lucky we found this one snoozing. Now we can see its four wings and the tops of its giant eyes.

Can you also see the rectangles on its long body?

Try It!

A rectangle has four sides: two long and two short. It also has four corners. Use your finger to trace the rectangle shape.

corner

long side

short side

rectangle

cone

Squirrels love pine cones.
The cone shape hides
seeds inside.
The squirrel <u>gobbles</u>
all the yummy seeds.
Then it drops the cone
to the forest floor.
Look out below!

Try It!

A cone shape looks like
a triangle and circle put
together. Trace the shapes
with your finger.

$$\triangle + \bigcirc = \triangle$$

The snail tiptoes up the plant. It is a quiet and strange beauty. One big foot. A pretty spiral shell. A little slime.

Why slime? The slime helps the snail stick so it can climb and hang.

Try It!

A spiral shape starts at the center and spins outward. Grab a piece of paper and draw your own!

spiral

ovoid

Baby birds wiggle inside blue oval eggs.

Wait!

It is not time to crack yet.
Mom just left to get
an earthworm snack.
She will be right back.

Try It!

If you stretch out a flat circle, you have an oval.

A solid oval is an ovoid. How many ovoids are in the nest?

Baby raccoons find something new. The fun <u>cylinder</u> shape of a log. One finds a place to climb. The other finds a hidey-hole.

Yawn, it is nap time. The raccoons now have a safe and warm place to sleep during a storm.

Try It!

A cylinder is a solid shape. It looks like a rectangle and a circle put together.

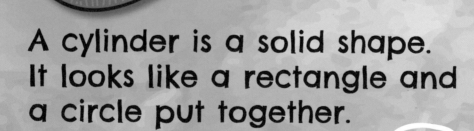

Find both shapes on the log.

cylinder

arc

Raindrops tap, tap, tap.

Look at the top of the mushroom. This shape is an <u>arc</u>. Under it is a great place to stay dry if you are very small.

Soon the rain clouds will roll away . . .

Try It!

An arc is part of a circle or curved line. Trace the arc and then the complete circle with your finger.

That's when the sun and the last of the rain make magic. Wow, look at that shape . . . A perfect arc of many colors—

a rainbow!

Shape Gallery

How many shapes can you find in these pictures?

Try It! Activities

In this book, readers learned about flat and solid shapes, and how different shapes can make other shapes. Here are a couple activities kids can do to practice their shape skills. Read kids the activities and help them take the fun beyond the pages of this book.

SILLY SPHERES (pages 6–7)

Basketballs, oranges, drops of water, and even doughnut holes are all spheres. But they don't stack easily. Try it with a friend. Grab a bunch of tennis balls. Take turns trying to pile up the balls to find out who can build the tallest tower in 15 seconds. Try it with triangle and cube-shaped blocks if you have them. Which shapes work best? Which are the most fun to pile up?

CUBE ART (page 12)

Turn ice cubes into art. With the help of an adult, mix different colors of washable paint (finger paint or tempera) with water and pour it into an ice cube tray. Let the cubes freeze. Use the colorful ice cubes to "draw" other shapes, including a rainbow.

SNAIL SPIRAL (pages 18–19)

Most snail shells spiral in a clockwise direction. But some spiral in the other direction. Just like some people are right-handed and some are left-handed. Try drawing snail spirals with your right hand. Then try with your left hand.

Glossary

arc (ahrk) A curved line between two points, usually part of a circle.

boulder (BOHL-dur) A large rock.

cardinal (KAHR-duh-nuhl) A songbird with black coloring around the beak and a crest of feathers on its head. The male is bright red.

cube (kyoob) A solid shape with six square sides.

cylinder (SIL-uhn-dur) A shape with flat, circular ends and sides shaped like the outside of a tube.

dew (doo) Moisture in the form of small drops that collects overnight on cool surfaces outside.

explore (ik-SPLOR) To travel and look around in order to discover things.

gobble (GAH-buhl) To eat food in a hurry.

hexagon (HEK-suh-gahn) A shape with six straight sides.

honeycomb (HUHN-ee-kohm) A wax structure made by bees to store honey and pollen, and provide a place to raise young bees. A honeycomb is made up of many rows of cells with six sides.

ovoid (OH-void) An egg shape or solid oval shape.

slime (slime) A moist, soft, and slippery substance usually thought of as unpleasant.

snooze (snooz) To sleep lightly and briefly, usually during the day; to doze.

solid (SAH-lid) A three-dimensional object or geometric figure. Spheres and cubes are solids.

sphere (sfeer) A solid form like that of a basketball or globe, with all points on the surface the same distance from the center.

spiral (SPYE-ruhl) Winding in a continuous curve around a fixed point or central axis, as in the spiral in a snail's shell.

stretch (strech) To extend or spread out over an area.

sway (sway) To move or swing slowly backward and forward or from side to side, as in flowers swaying in the wind.

Index

Page numbers in **bold** indicate illustrations.

ABOUT THE AUTHOR

Ruth A. Musgrave loves exploring forests, the ocean, and anywhere else outdoors. She shares her love of animals and nature through her books and articles. She is the author of thirty-five books, including *Mission: Shark Rescue* and BBC Earth's *Do You Know? Animal Sounds.*